IACOBVS.QVINTVS.SCOTTORVM.REX   MARIA.LOTHORINGIA.ILLIVS.IN.SECVNDIS.NVP

ANNO.ÆTATIS.SVE.   TIIS VXOR. ANNO ÆTATIS SVE. Z 4

MARY QUEEN OF SCOTS

FRONT COVER: *Mary Queen of Scots as remembered by later ages : a lonely figure in black velvet dress, her face saddened by misfortune and long captivity. A portrait of c. 1610, after Hilliard, detail from the painting in the National Portrait Gallery.*

BACK COVER: *The memorial portrait of Mary Queen of Scots, now at Blairs College, was commissioned by her devoted lady-in-waiting Elizabeth Curle, who received the queen's last kiss before dying.*

ABOVE: *Mary's parents: James V of Scotland, who died heartbroken that his newborn heir was a "lass"; and Mary of Guise, who sent Mary to France for her education while she governed Scotland in her name.*

MARY QUEEN OF SCOTS

G W O WOODWARD

BEFORE she was a week old, Mary Stewart was queen of Scotland. She was born in the royal palace of Linlithgow on 8 December 1542. Six days later, at Falkland, her father king James V died, it is said, of despair at the crumbling fortunes of his kingdom and family. A few days earlier the Scottish army had been soundly beaten by the English at Solway Moss. Many of the Scottish nobles were prisoners in the hands of the belligerent and ambitious English king Henry VIII, and it seemed that once again, as after Flodden nearly thirty years before, Scotland was at the mercy of her southern neighbour.

This national disaster was bad enough, but for king James there was the added bitterness of domestic disappointments. Though the sons which he had fathered outside marriage seemed healthy and sturdy enough, the only two his wife had borne him had died in early infancy, and now his third legitimate child had proved to be a girl. In that masculine age an heiress was a liability rather than an asset to a ruling house. Even if her sex did not bar her altogether from the throne (as it would have done in France) she would inevitably be the focus of intense domestic and international rivalry as ambitious nobles and princes vied for her hand in marriage and for the control of her kingdom that would go with it. Her very existence would provoke discord and strife and weaken the authority of the throne she occupied.

*   *   *

And so it was to be with Mary. Married three times, none of her marriages were to last very long, and during girlhood and widowhood she was repeatedly beset by the intrigues of rival suitors, spurred on, despite her generally acknowledged feminine charm, more often by ambition than devotion. For not only was Mary, almost from birth, the queen of one kingdom in her own right, she also had a very important dynastic link with the English royal house which might one day bring her to a second and more important throne. Her father's mother had been Margaret Tudor, daughter of Henry VII and elder sister of Henry VIII. If the latter's heirs should fail, the Scottish royal house stood next in line to England.

However in 1542 this was a rather remote prospect. Henry VIII's three children, Edward, Mary and Elizabeth, were all alive and would surely between them provide sufficient heirs to bar the Scottish claim. It was only as the years went by and first Edward (1547–53) and then Mary Tudor (1553–58) ruled England and died without offspring that Scottish Mary's English ancestry became a matter of immediate concern in international politics.

For the first six years of the young queen's life those who contested the control of her person and destiny were more immediately interested in her Scottish kingdom than in her long-term chances of the English throne. The two chief rivals in the field were the rulers of France and England. Henry VIII was the first to act. Eager to subject Scotland permanently to his authority, and in a position, so he thought, to dictate terms, he proposed a marriage between his young son Edward, now aged five, and the new-born Scottish queen. When Edward eventually succeeded his father in England the two thrones would be united. Meanwhile Mary would be brought to England and Henry would govern Scotland in her name. In this way centuries of Anglo-Scottish feuding would be brought to an end, and the northern frontier of England made secure. The captive Scottish nobles at Henry's court had little option but to agree to this proposal, but on their release and return home they swiftly changed their minds. They had no desire to see their beloved country made an English province. Stubbornly they resisted all Henry's blandishments and threats. Mary was kept out of his hands, but Scotland had to fight for her independence.

The natural alternative to an English marriage for Mary was a French one. The "auld alliance" between France and Scotland was of long standing and rested on the very firm foundation of a shared desire to check the expansionist ambitions of the English kings. Mary's own mother, Mary of Guise, was herself a symbol of this alliance. She came of a family which, though it was not French in origin, had risen high in fortune and influence in France. Francis, duke of Guise, and Charles, cardinal of Lorraine, young Mary's uncles, were soon to be the leading men in that country. They sought to raise the fortunes of their family still further by marrying their little Scottish niece into the French royal house. Henry II, who became king of France in

1547, readily fell in with the Guise family schemes and offered as bridegroom his own eldest son, the dauphin Francis, two years Mary's junior. A dynastic union such as this would make permanent the political link with Scotland and very effectively keep England in check. Later, when the childless deaths of Edward VI and Mary Tudor brought the Scottish Mary closer to the English throne, the plans of French king Henry II were to grow more ambitious, as we shall see.

From the Scottish point of view a union of the French and Scottish thrones would as effectively subject Scotland to an alien power as would a union with England, but in the 1540s subjection to the old ally France seemed preferable to subjection to the old enemy England, and so the French marriage was agreed to and the young queen of Scotland was sent to France.

Thus ended the first turbulent chapter in young Mary's life. When she sailed from Dumbarton on 7 August 1548 she was not yet six years old, and can have had very little notion of the bitterness of the struggles that had raged around her almost

since her birth. She had lived most of her life within the shelter of the sturdy walls of Stirling castle, out of reach of English armies, and protected too from intriguing nobles while her mother fought for the right to govern Scotland in her name and rival ambassadors contended for her future.

The next ten years were comparatively uneventful. Mary grew to maturity in the sheltered environment of the French royal nursery, the daily playmate and constant companion of her young husband-designate. Much of her time was spent at the palace of Fontainebleau, or at the great royal chateaux on the Loire, Blois and Chambord. Her days passed pleasantly with schooling interspersed with games and outdoor recreations. It was probably during these years that she acquired her lifelong passion for the chase.

During these same years her future seemed secure. When they were old enough she would marry Francis, for whom she early developed a deep, but probably sisterly, affection. In due course, when his father died, he would be king and she would be queen of France. Scotland, that remote northern

land of which she was already titular queen, was probably very seldom in her thoughts.

In 1558 events began to move again. In April, when she was not yet sixteen, and he was barely fourteen, Francis and Mary were married in Notre Dame in Paris. In November, when Mary Tudor died in England, the French king, Henry II, arguing, with some justification, that her half-sister Elizabeth, being the offspring of the bigamous marriage of Henry VIII and Anne Boleyn, was illegitimate and could not inherit the English throne, advanced the claim of his recently acquired daughter-in-law, the young queen of Scotland, to be also queen of England in succession to her lately deceased cousin and namesake. In July of the following year king Henry died from wounds inflicted accidentally in a "friendly" bout of jousting and Mary of Scotland now reached the pinnacle of her regal career as queen in three kingdoms; queen-regnant of Scotland; queen-consort of France; queen-claimant of England.

This early challenge by Mary to Elizabeth I's position is important in helping to explain the English queen's later attitude to her Scottish cousin. It matters little that the initiative in putting forward Mary's claim to be not just next heir to Elizabeth but rightfully queen of England in her place, came originally from the French king, and that Mary, a little over a year and a half later, was content enough to acknowledge Elizabeth's title and to seek no more than recognition as her heir. Elizabeth could never forget this initial attempt to

*   *   *

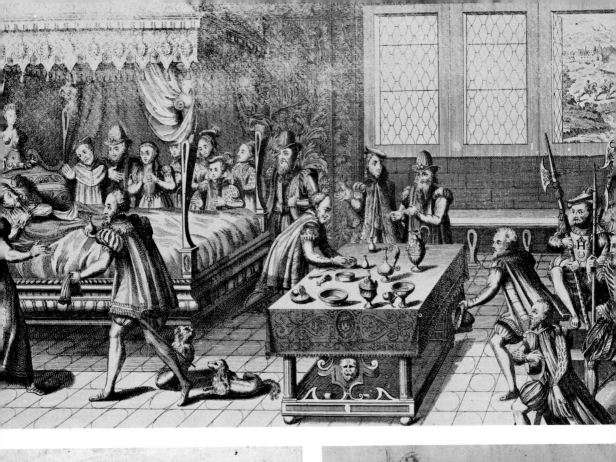

exclude her from her father's throne. While Mary lived there was always the chance that someone would press her claims again. Mary was a standing threat to Elizabeth's personal security.

Mary did not long enjoy her triple queenship. In July 1560, by the treaty of Edinburgh, she was required to abandon her claim to be queen of England. In December of the same year her weakly husband died from an uncontrolled infection of the ear and was succeeded by his younger brother Charles. As a childless widow Mary was now of no account in France. All that was left to her was her original Scottish throne.

But Scotland itself had undergone a revolution. In 1559, in the name of the reformed religion, and aided by the fiery preaching of John Knox, and by arms and money from England, a group of Scottish nobles, the self-styled Lords of the Congregation, had overthrown the government of the regent, Mary's mother. They had then summoned the Scottish parliament and remodelled the Scottish church on Protestant lines. What sort of reception would these new masters of the Scottish kingdom give to the eighteen-year-old queen in whose name they still professed to govern, she who had been brought up at the French court, firm in the traditional Catholic faith? It says a great deal for Mary's courage that she was prepared to put this question to the test. On 14 August 1561 she sailed from Calais and returned to Scotland which she had not seen for thirteen years.

Her people received her at first with caution, and then with growing pleas-

*   *   *

FACING PAGE (above): *The French royal family gathers round the deathbed of Henry II mortally wounded in a joust. Mary is seen (in profile) by the right-hand bedpost next to Francis. A 16th-century woodcut.*

FACING PAGE (below left): *A study of Mary aged 16 by Clouet: she is dressed in mourning for her father-in-law, whose death left her queen of France.*

FACING PAGE (below right): *Francis, the sickly dauphin, who was Mary's "sweetheart and friend". He married Mary in 1558 but died just over two years later.*

RIGHT: *Henry Stewart, Lord Darnley, at the age of 17, with his younger brother Charles. This portrait by Hans Eworth may have been intended to attract prospective brides.*

ure. Her good looks and stately bearing (she was notably tall for a woman in her generation) won their hearts, her tragic young widowhood aroused their compassion, her moderation overcame their fears. Though she quietly insisted in face of the fulminations of Knox upon her right to worship in her own way, she was plainly no crusading Catholic bigot come to sweep away the recent reformation. And she soon had allies among the ruling lords.

One of the leaders of the Lords of the Congregation was Mary's illegitimate half-brother, the Lord James Stewart, better known by his later title of earl of Moray. In the initial stages of the negotiations for the queen's return to Scotland he had a prominent part to play. He visited her in France and impressed upon her the need to accept the recent religious changes in her kingdom. At the same time he spoke out strongly for her own right, if she so wished, to continue to hear masses in the privacy of her royal chapel, and established with Mary a mutual confidence which was to be the foundation upon which her early successes in Scotland were to rest. For Mary was at first a great success. The invective of Knox, who was quite incapable of extending to her religious views the degree of tolerance she accorded his, and the shadows of later disasters tend too often to obscure the fact that for the first few years after her return to Scotland in 1561 Mary played the very difficult role of Catholic queen in a recently protestantised country with tact, with charm and with energy. She also, though she was still little more than a girl, managed to keep a very effective check upon the ambitions and rivalries of her quarrelsome and turbulent nobles. In this latter task the support of Lord James, twelve years her senior, was invaluable.

And yet, however successful she may have been in tackling the many problems that beset her as queen, there was one that she most lamentably failed to solve, and that was the question of her marriage. She would, of course, have to take a husband. No woman could rule alone. (Elizabeth I had not yet been long enough on the throne of England to prove the exception to that current generalisation.) Every queen needed the strength and support of a husband to uphold her authority in what was very definitely a man's job in a man's world. It was, of course, also the duty of every queen to provide for the future security of her kingdom by producing an heir. The question therefore was not "Should Mary marry?" but "Whom should she marry?"

Nor was this a question that affected Mary and Scotland alone. England and Elizabeth were also deeply concerned about it. While Elizabeth remained unmarried Mary had a very strong claim to be acknowledged as her heir, and so the man Mary married might one day be not only king of Scotland but king of England, or at least, the father of an English king. Elizabeth in fact never openly accepted Mary as her heir, for there were other claimants to be considered and as a matter of policy the English queen preferred to keep the question open. But it was clear from the close interest that she took in the problem of finding a husband for Mary that Elizabeth did regard this as a matter of major moment for her subjects and herself.

For Mary's hand there was no shortage of suitors. As queen of one country with a good claim to be heir to another she was the best available bargain in the international marriage market. Spanish and Imperial princes were strongly fancied, but Elizabeth disapproved. Alien princes meant alien influences, and alien influences (other than English) in Scotland were to be discouraged. As an alternative candidate Elizabeth, somewhat surprisingly, and at first a little coyly, suggested her own first favourite, Robert Dudley, now raised to the peerage as earl of Leicester to make him more acceptable. But Mary would have none of him. Continued on page 14

* * *

LEFT (above): *James Stewart, earl of Moray and Mary's half-brother, became her trusted adviser.* (Below) *George Buchanan, poet and scholar, wrote plays and verses to entertain Mary's carefree court.*

FACING PAGE (top): *The Queen's Outer Chamber where David Riccio's lacerated body was left by his murderers, traditionally at the spot marked by the brass plate on the floor.*

FACING PAGE (below left): *The oak coffered ceiling in Queen Mary's bedroom at Holyroodhouse, showing the carved initials of Mary's parents. This room was linked by a private staircase to Lord Darnley's room beneath* (below right).

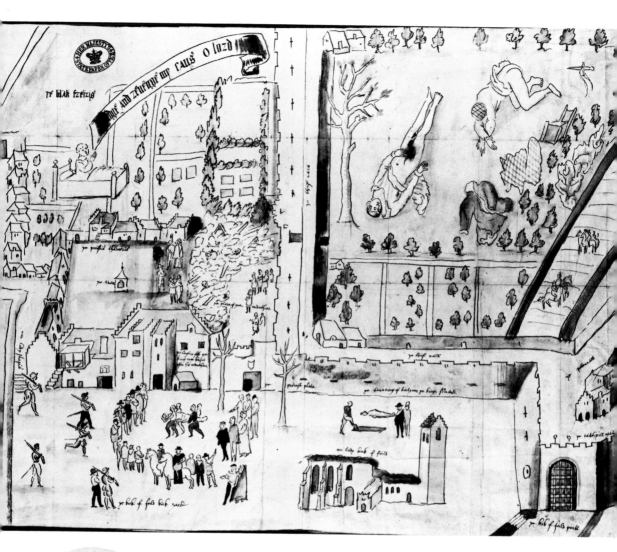

FACING PAGE: *Mary was married to Lord Darnley in the chapel royal at Holyrood on 29 July 1565. This print of Mary and her new husband was based on an original painting by Elstraak.*

LEFT: *David Riccio, Mary's Italian secretary, was one of the "sly crafty foreigners" hated by the Scottish nobles for their intimacy with the queen. Riccio was a talented poet and musician and used to play cards with Mary late into the night, and so earned the jealousy of her husband, Lord Darnley. On the evening of 9 March 1566 as Mary dined with a few friends in the supper room, Darnley and his supporters burst in and seized Riccio. He was dragged screaming through the door and stabbed to death in the audience chamber beyond. As the alarm was given the murderers dropped their victim's body and fled. Lord Darnley's*

dagger was left by the corpse to prove his involvement in the brutal deed. He himself was murdered less than a year later.

ABOVE: *A contemporary sketch of the scene on the outskirts of Edinburgh after Lord Darnley's murder, 10 February 1567. The explosion that startled the city in the early hours had left the house at Kirk o' Field where Darnley had been staying a heap of rubble (centre of picture). The bodies of Darnley and his servant were found under a tree just outside the city walls (top right); they had been strangled while escaping from the house before the gunpowder exploded. A group of guards and bystanders watch Darnley's body borne to the new provost's lodgings (bottom left). Little James, seven-month-old son of Mary and Darnley, is shown in his cradle (top left).*

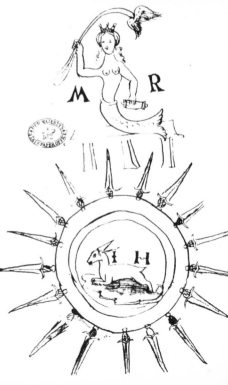

FACING PAGE (top): *Hermitage Castle, Roxburghshire. When Bothwell lay wounded in this border fortress in October 1566, Mary rode over 40 miles to visit him and returned to Jedburgh the same day.*

FACING PAGE (below left): *The only known portrait of James Hepburn, earl of Bothwell. A violent, ambitious nobleman, he aimed at replacing Darnley as the queen's consort. Later, witnesses accused him of having personally set light to the gunpowder under Darnley's rooms. A few months after the murder, he abducted Mary and married her.*

FACING PAGE (below right): *This propaganda placard appeared in Edinburgh soon after Darnley's murder. It shows Mary as a mermaid (prostitute), above a hare (Bothwell's family crest) surrounded by daggers—an attempt by Mary's enemies to link her name to the murder.*

BELOW: *James VI as a child. Though shown here with a hawk, James was fonder of his books; he grew up to hate his mother Mary as a murderess.*

RIGHT: *A full length portrait of Mary, painted during her long captivity in England. It is now in the collection of Lord Salisbury at Hatfield House.*

In the end Mary herself chose to marry Henry Lord Darnley, eldest son and heir of the earl of Lennox, and her own first cousin. It would appear, on Mary's part, to have been a genuine love match. So captivated was she by his outward charm that she totally failed to see behind it to the shallow self-indulgent and ambitious character that his attractive exterior concealed.

The Darnley marriage was Mary's great mistake and the beginning of her tragic downfall. Outwardly the young man, who was nearer to her in age than any of the other candidates for her hand, had everything to recommend him. He came of royal lineage on both sides. His mother, born Margaret Douglas, was a daughter of Mary's grandmother, Margaret Tudor, by a second marriage. His father was descended from a junior branch of the royal house of Stewart. His claim to the English throne was almost as good as Mary's and was immeasurably strengthened by his marriage to her.

Their son was James VI who was eventually to follow Elizabeth on the English throne.

But Darnley was young and spoiled by an ambitious mother. He lacked the strength of character and was incapable of the selfless devotion to his wife's interests which was so necessary to help her through the difficult situation resulting from the jealousies which her marriage so naturally produced. Indeed his pride and insensitivity only served to aggravate a situation which would have been difficult enough without them. And in the end his gullibility made him the easy victim of ruthless men's intrigues.

The most immediate and serious consequence of Mary's marriage to Darnley at Holyrood on 29 July 1565 was that it broke the working partnership between herself and Moray. He who had supported her so faithfully since her return to Scotland, and who had become, because of the high esteem in which the queen held

him, virtually the first man in the kingdom, now found himself pushed aside in favour of the new young king, a callow, selfish youth, who was, moreover, the son of Moray's ancient

*   *   *

ABOVE: *Lord Darnley's family pray at his tomb for God to avenge his murder. The painting, by Vogelarius is dated 1567 and the setting is probably imaginary. The effigy of Darnley rests on the tomb decorated with family crests and scenes of his murder. Inscriptions recount his virtues and his untimely death. Darnley's father, the earl of Lennox, was in no doubt who was guilty and brought a private lawsuit against Bothwell. Their prayers were answered when four months later Lennox and the confederate lords defeated Bothwell at Carberry Hill and Mary was taken prisoner. This is recorded in the bottom left hand corner of the picture above. A contemporary sketch of the event was also made (facing page). Mary has just surrendered and is being led across to her enemies (see left).*

rival, Lennox. Moray sulked, and then went into rebellion, was outlawed and fled to England.

It was not easy for Mary to find a substitute for Moray. Darnley was not the man to counsel or advise. Interested only in the power and opportunities his newly-acquired royalty gave him, he had no thought for the responsibilities which his position involved. Nor could any other Scottish noble measure up to the stature of Moray, and, in any case, since even Moray had let her down, Mary was less inclined to put her trust in any other. Inevitably she came to rely more and more upon the advice and assistance of her professional staff, her secretaries and household officers, and in particular upon that of her Italian secretary David Riccio.

The love affair with Darnley did not last. Mary's pregnancy contributed to its ending. The physical discomfort she endured was not compensated for by any increase in husbandly concern. When she could no longer ride or hunt he continued to pursue such pleasures on his own. The blindfold of infatuation was lifted from her eyes. She saw him now for what he was, a self-indulgent playboy, given over too frequently to drink and other excesses. Mary ceased even to delight in his company on the rare occasions when he offered it. Estrangement grew between them as rapidly as the original affair.

Darnley, for his part, grew suspicious. His wife no longer doted on him. She no longer lavished gifts upon him, or pandered to his whims. She kept the exercise of the regal power increasingly to herself, though earlier she had been eager to associate him as king with her in all her acts. It was easy in these circumstances for jealous nobles, plotting mischief, to focus Darnley's attention upon Riccio who seemed now to be so well established in the confidence of the queen, and to persuade him to give his full support to the plot they were hatching to assassinate the Italian secretary.

On the night of 9 March 1566, while Mary sat at supper in Holyrood house, Darnley unexpectedly entered the queen's apartments by means of the private stairway from his own suite on the floor below. Hardly had the queen's party, which included Riccio, recovered from this unlooked for intrusion when the other conspirators followed by the same route, seized the secretary, dragged him struggling and protesting from the room and savagely stabbed him to death outside. The motives of the participants in this violent deed were varied. For Darnley it was a comparatively straightforward act of vengeance against the man who, he believed, had supplanted him in the queen's affections. For others of the murderers the victim was a low-born upstart who had risen too high in the kingdom and was ousting better men from the positions of influence to which their birth entitled them. Some

perhaps even entertained the hope that the shock of their barbarous deed would cause Mary, who was six months pregnant, to miscarry and even to die, leaving the way clear for Darnley to claim the kingdom in his own right. Thereafter they could hope to share in the spoils and to rule the kingdom through their influence over him. Mary herself chose to believe afterwards that her own life had been directly aimed at. For this she never forgave Darnley, though she appeared for a while to forget.

The murder of Riccio solved nothing. The gulf between Mary and Darnley grew even wider as she learned more fully of the extent of his complicity in the crime. The disaffected nobles who had hoped to profit with Darnley from the elimination of the Italian were soon as anxious to be rid in turn of him and his pretensions. He was an embarrassment to all parties including the queen. His private life became if anything more scandalous and dissolute. Some-

thing would have to be done about him. But at first Mary concealed the depth of her revulsion from her husband until the child she bore him had been born. For the future security of her throne and kingdom it was vital that neither the life nor the legitimacy of that child should be put at risk.

Prince James, Mary's only child, and Darnley's son, was born on 19 June 1566. When Mary had recovered from the birth, and from the nearly fatal illness that afflicted her a few months later, she was readier to act. With a party of nobles (which included Moray, now restored to favour, and Bothwell, whose staunch support at the time of Riccio's murder had been invaluable to her) Mary, in late November, discussed the problem of her husband. The possibility of divorce was raised, and dark hints dropped of "other means". There is, however, no certain evidence that Mary was at any time a party to the plans that now began to be laid against the life of Darnley, but neither

is there any positive evidence that she was not. The whole affair of Darnley's death is one of the most intractable mysteries of history, and every

Continued on page 21

* * *

ABOVE: *A panel of embroidery, now at Oxburgh Hall, Norfolk, believed to have been embroidered by Mary and "Bess of Hardwick", showing numerous devices and anagrams often of her own name which Mary liked to incorporate in her work.*

FACING PAGE (above): *Elisabeth Hardwick, better known as "Bess of Hardwick" (left), was the wife of Mary's keeper, George, earl of Shrewsbury (right). He kept Mary in custody on his estates in Derbyshire from 1569–84, and liked to show her off to visitors, even being falsely accused by Bess of having an affair with her.*

FACING PAGE (below): *The "Blairs Jewel" contains a miniature of Mary from a portrait painted during her captivity. Such miniatures were distributed to Mary's Catholic supporters in Britain and abroad.*

GEORGIVS TALBOTVS
COMES SALOPIÆ
AN·ÆTATIS·58
S·H
1580

Al pensier che mi nuoce insieme e giova
Amaro e dolce al mio cor cangia spesso
E fra tema e speranza lo tien sì oppresso
Che la quiete pace unque nò trova.

Però, se questa carta à voi rinnova
Il bel disio di vedervi in me impresso
Ciò fa il grand'affanno ch'in se stesso
Ha, non potendo homai da se far prova.

Ho veduto talhor vicino al porto
Rispinger nave in mar contrario vento
E nel maggior seren' turbarsi il Cielo

Così sorella chiara temo e pavento
Non gia per noi, ma quante volte à torto
Rompe fortuna un ben' ordito velo.

FACING PAGE: *For 14 of the 18 years which she spent in confinement in England, Mary was the "guest" of the earl and countess of Shrewsbury, who usually resided at Sheffield Castle (above). In January 1585 she was removed to Tutbury (below), in the more rigorous care of Sir Amyas Paulet.*

ABOVE: *Mary composed this elegant sonnet in Italian to Elizabeth after her flight to England in 1568. In it she asks for a personal interview; an English translation reads as follows:*

A longing haunts my spirit day and night
Bitter and sweet, torments my aching heart
Between doubt and fear, it holds its wayward part,
And while it lingers, rest and peace take flight.
Dear sister, if these lines too boldly speak
Of my fond wish to see you, 'tis for this—
That I repine and sink in bitterness,
If still denied the favour that I seek.
I have seen a ship freed from control
On the high seas, outside a friendly port,
And what was peaceful change to woe and pain;
Even so am I, a lonely, trembling soul,
Fearing—not you, but to be made the sport
Of Fate, that bursts the closest, strongest chain.

ABOVE (right): *Elizabeth I of England.*

RIGHT: *The exquisite silver casket in Lennoxlove Museum is believed to have contained the ill-famed "Casket Letters" —love letters said to have been written by Mary to Bothwell.*

19

ABOVE (left): *William Cecil, Lord Burghley, led the prosecution at Mary's trial and secured her conviction.*

★

ABOVE (right): *Sir Francis Walsingham, head of Elizabeth's secret service, intercepted Mary's letters to Anthony Babington, a Catholic conspirator.*

★

RIGHT: *Thomas Howard, duke of Norfolk, rashly planned to marry Mary in 1569–70, for which he was imprisoned. He was executed in 1572 for treason.*

★

FACING PAGE: *The layout of Mary's trial at Fotheringhay Castle, 15 October 1586. Mary sat on a chair in the right of the room. The court consisted of earls (sitting on the left bench) and barons and knights of the Privy Council (right and centre benches).*

account of it leaves some loose ends. Even the way he died is not quite clear. The house, at Kirk o' Field in Edinburgh, in which he was resident on the night of 9–10 February 1567, was totally destroyed by an explosion at 2 a.m., but Darnley's body was found in a garden on the other side of the town wall, strangled!

What matters to Mary's story is not how Darnley died, or who killed him, but what her contemporaries believed at the time. Popular report ascribed the leadership in the conspiracy against Darnley to James Hepburn, earl of Bothwell. When, therefore, a bare three months after the murder, on 15 May 1567 Mary married this same Bothwell Scotland was scandalised. And even those of Bothwell's former fellow conspirators who were not scandalised were nevertheless taken aback. If they could have foreseen that the elimination of Darnley would only lead to the promotion of Bothwell to his place, they would not have joined so willingly in the plot. And so it was not long before yet another conspiracy was formed, this time to "free" the queen from Bothwell.

In contrast to the previous plots, this one had widespread support. The public reputation of the queen had been tarnished beyond recovery by her third marriage. Many of her people were quite ready now to believe that she had actually and deliberately participated in the plot against Darnley in order to clear the way for Bothwell. Some were beginning to wonder if there would ever be peace in Scotland with this shameless woman on the throne there to invite conspiracy, intrigue and murder. Others began to think that the infant James might offer a better alternative. If he could be set up as king and a regency established to rule in his name, there might be some hope of achieving stability.

This was the plan eventually adopted by the group of Scottish nobles who "rescued" Mary from Bothwell at Carberry Hill on 15 June 1567, and then very promptly shut her up a prisoner in lonely Lochleven castle. There they forced her to sign a deed of abdication, and to name a council of regency for her infant son.

On 29 July 1567 James VI was crowned king at Stirling, and in August Mary's half-brother Moray was proclaimed regent. Moray thus

appears to be the ultimate beneficiary of all the conspiracies and murders of the preceding two years. He had discreetly avoided direct involvement in both the Riccio and the Darnley affairs, and had even more discreetly retired to England during the rise and fall of Bothwell. Now he returned to assume a position of power even greater than that he had enjoyed as Mary's confidant before Darnley had come on the scene. From 1567 to 1570, when he in turn fell to an assassin's bullet, he brought to Scotland an unaccustomed continuity in government.

Bothwell escaped capture in Scot-land, but was forced to flee abroad. He went to Norway and was arrested and imprisoned by the king of Denmark. The rigours of his imprisonment drove him out of his mind and he died insane in 1578.

Mary's imprisonment in Lochleven lasted less than a year. On 2 May 1568, with the aid of sympathisers within the castle, she escaped and made a desperate bid to regain her throne. Defeated by the forces of the regent at Langside on 13 May she fled first to Dumfries and then across the Solway Firth to England, landing at Workington on 16 May.

Mary never set foot in Scotland

again, but her cause there was not immediately lost. Her partisans and those of the young king and his regents kept up a spasmodic civil conflict which was eventually ended in favour of the latter by active English intervention in 1573. For several years after her flight Mary's restoration was not too remote a possibility, but one that would depend very much upon the attitude adopted by the English queen who now found herself faced with the problem of dealing with an uninvited and embarrassing royal guest.

Elizabeth's attitude to Mary was the product of conflicting impulses. The one object she had clearly in mind at all times was the need to keep Scotland free from any undesirable alien influences. England's security was Elizabeth's first concern. Mary, who was so ready to appeal to the pope, to the king of France or to the king of Spain for help in recovering her throne, and who might still be persuaded to press her claim to England was, from Elizabeth's point of view, a less desirable occupant of the Scottish throne than young James and his protecting lords who relied so heavily on English support to maintain themselves and their authority. But, on the other hand, Mary was rightful queen of Scotland and Elizabeth could hardly approve of her deposition by her own subjects. That sort of precedent was not to be encouraged.

At one point, in October 1568, it looked as if Elizabeth was seeking a way out when she permitted representatives of the Scottish lords to participate in an enquiry into Darnley's death which was held by English commissioners, acting in their own queen's name, at York. If Mary was shown to have been a consenting party to the murder, perhaps then Elizabeth would accept the justice of her deposition. It was at this investigation that the famous silver casket, allegedly containing incriminating letters from Mary to Bothwell, was first produced. Elizabeth was not very much impressed by these, but did realise thereafter that the Scottish lords were determined to convict Mary and that if she were permitted to return to Scotland it would be almost certainly to trial, condemnation and execution. If, on the other hand, Elizabeth set Mary free and allowed her to go to France or Spain to seek support, she would be actively encouraging foreign intervention in Scotland of the kind she was anxious above all to avoid.

And so Mary remained for 18 years in forced residence in England, not so much as a consequence of a deliberate act of policy on Elizabeth's part but rather because the English queen could never find a satisfactory way out of her dilemma. Mary's residences were many; Carlisle, Bolton, Chatsworth, Sheffield, South Wingfield, Coventry, Tutbury, Chartley and, finally Fotheringhay. The conditions of her detention also varied. For many years her custodian, at Sheffield, Chatsworth and Wingfield, was the earl of Shrewsbury whose domineering wife, Bess of Hardwick, accused him of dangerous leniency towards his charge, allowing her to take exercise abroad, to court popularity by distributing alms to the local poor, and even to take the waters at Buxton. On other occasions, especially at Tutbury, she was much more strictly confined, her attendants reduced in number, her correspondence censored and access to her person rigorously controlled. At times like this she was much more of a prisoner than an honoured guest.

Throughout the long years of her imprisonment Mary never gave up hope of securing her release. Repeat-

*   *   *

LEFT: *The scene in the hall at Fotheringhay castle on 8 February 1587, recorded in a contemporary sketch. A large crowd had come that cold winter morning to watch Mary's execution; she is shown entering (top left), and being disrobed on the central stage.*

FACING PAGE (above): *A detail from the memorial portrait of Mary at Blairs College (see back cover) recaptures the actual moment of her beheading, watched by English nobles and officials. The executioner took three blows to sever her neck.*

FACING PAGE (below): *This gold rosary and prayer book carried by Mary at her execution were given to one of Mary's friends, wife of Philip, earl of Arundel. They are still in the possession of his descendant, the duke of Norfolk, and are on view at Arundel Castle.*

edly she asked for a personal interview with Elizabeth, confident that such a confrontation would swiftly resolve all difficulties and win Elizabeth's unqualified support. But Elizabeth steadily ignored her pleas and the two queens never met. In her very natural eagerness to be free Mary was willing to accept the aid of almost anyone prepared to offer it, and this lack of caution in her dealings with would-be rescuers was to be her ruin in the end.

The whole period of her imprisonment was punctuated by plots on her behalf. Some of the conspirators, such as the group of local Derbyshire and Lancashire gentry who planned to spirit her away from Chatsworth in 1570, were moved more by romance or hope of immediate reward than by any deep-seated religious or political motivation. But other plots, especially those hatched after the papal bull excommunicating and deposing Elizabeth in May 1570, had more dangerous international ramifications. When pope Pius V decided at long last to move against Elizabeth since there seemed no hope remaining that she would seek an accommodation with Rome, the rightful queen of England both in foreign and in native Catholic eyes, was now the captive Mary. From then on most of the plots involving her had the same purpose, and only the details varied. They all envisaged the elimination of Elizabeth, the release of Mary and her elevation to the English throne. Some schemes also included the marriage of Mary to some suitable Catholic prince or noble. The more dangerous of the plots also involved the invasion of England by a foreign force, usually Spanish. None of these conspiracies was in itself really serious. Most of them were uncovered in good time, but their effect was cumulative. The more often the queen of Scots was shown to be the focus for subversion, the more eagerly Elizabeth's loyal subjects pressed for her elimination. The more frequent the plots the more difficult it was for Elizabeth to resist the pressure on her to act. In 1572, after the discovery of the Ridolphi plot and the execution of the duke of Norfolk, parliament urged Elizabeth to put Mary on trial for her part in the schemes of the plotters. Elizabeth was able to resist the pressure then, but 14 years later, in the very similar circumstances of the Babington conspiracy, she could not. In 1585 Parliament passed an act making mandatory the

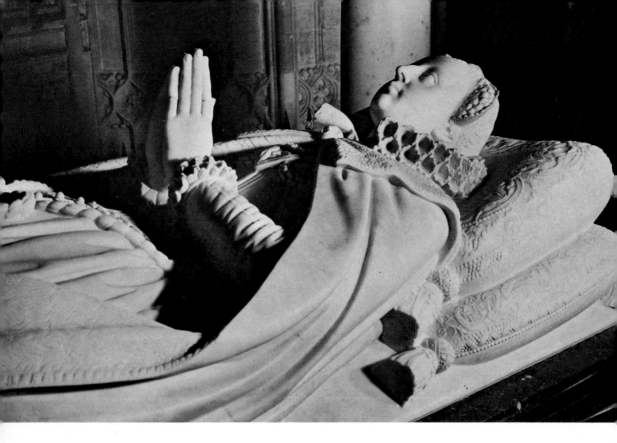

trial of any person on whose behalf a plot against the queen's life might be devised. Mary had to be tried, and the evidence of her complicity brought forward at her trial could not be ignored. Her conviction followed swiftly, and only the queen's clemency could then save her from the sentence of death that the court imposed.

Yet still Elizabeth hesitated to take any irreversible action. Only under pressure from her councillors did she permit a warrant for Mary's execution to be prepared. Only under pressure did she sign it. And only, according to her own account, against her will and without her knowledge was that warrant finally dispatched and acted on. The axe rose and fell, and Mary was no more. Elizabeth had sought to avoid responsibility for her death, but in the end it was under her authority that the queen of Scotland died.

* * *

ABOVE: *The effigy of Mary Queen of Scots on her tomb in Westminster Abbey, set up by James I. The features, serene and composed, were probably based on her death mask.*

Historical Links

Time has erased many of the castles and palaces that Mary knew. The sombre castle of Fotheringhay, Northants, where Mary died, is now a mound where thistles grow. Others are in ruins or have been transformed by later owners. But still the royal palaces of Linlithgow, Mary's birthplace, and Falkland, as well as noble seats such as Blair Castle, Traquair House and Lennoxlove House, are rich in associations with Mary's legend. These are open to the public.

Then there are the houses in England where Mary was imprisoned: Chatsworth, Derbyshire, has changed much since her time, but both here and at Hardwick Hall nearby there are many reminders of her long years of captivity. At Hatfield House there is a valuable collection of Mary's letters and other documents. All places are open to the public.

Peterborough Cathedral also has strong ties with her. After her execution at Fotheringhay Mary was buried in the presbytery there. In 1612 her son James I ordered that her body be removed and re-buried in Westminster Abbey.

But it is at the palace of Holyroodhouse, Edinburgh, that the links with the past are most vividly preserved. Visitors can see Mary's audience chamber, scene of violent arguments between her and Knox, and of the murder of Riccio; her bedroom; and the supper room where Riccio was dragged to his death.

*

ACKNOWLEDGMENTS

The illustrations are acknowledged as follows: pp 7, 9, 14, from the Royal Collection and reproduced by gracious permission of H.M. The Queen; pp 20 (below), 23 (below), by permission of His Grace the Duke of Norfolk; p 19 (bottom), The Duke of Hamilton and Brandon; pp 1, 16, 17 (top), The National Trust; pp i cover, 13 (left), 19 (top right), 20 (top), The National Portrait Gallery, London; p 2, J. Pugh; p 3, Musee Conde, Chantilly; p 4, Scottish Records Office; p 5 (top), French Tourist Board; p 5 (bottom), Photo Giraudon; pp 6 (top), 11 (below), 18 (bottom), 19 (top left), 21, 22, British Museum, by permission of the Trustees; p 6 (below left), Bibliotheque Nationale; p 6 (below right), Roger Viollet; pp 8, 12 (below left), Scottish National Portrait Gallery; p 9 (above) by Alastair Hunter; p 10, Mansell Collection; pp 11, 12, (right), 15, Public Records Office, Crown Copyright; p 12 (top), Department of the Environment; p 13 (right), Hatfield House, by permission of Lord Salisbury; p 18 (top), by permission of Sheffield City Libraries; pp 17 (bottom), 23 (top), iv cover, The Trustees of Blairs College, Aberdeen; p 24, S. W. Newbury, Hon. F.I.I.P., F.R.P.S., by permission of the Dean and Chapter, Westminster Abbey.

SBN 85372 074 6